Preface to Third Edition

The success of the first (1990) and second (1993) editions has shown the need for a booklet like this, covering both the organisation of the Criminal Justice System in England and Wales and the main procedures used within the system. It has proved useful both to those new to criminal justice and those wishing to extend their knowledge of the system. Versions have been reproduced in French and Polish, to enable foreign countries to compare the system in England and Wales with their own.

This edition is revised to include changes resulting from the Criminal Justice and Public Order Act 1994 and the Police and Magistrates' Courts Act 1994. It is intended to issue further editions, following substantial new legislation or administrative changes within our criminal justice system.

The author would like to thank all those colleagues within the Home Office, Lord Chancellor's Department and Crown Prosecution Service, who assisted in preparing this edition.

Comments are welcome and should be addressed to the author at Home Office, Lunar House, 40 Wellesley Road, Croydon, Surrey, CR0 9YD, to whom also any requests for further copies should be made.

Gordon C Barclay
March 1995

CONTENTS

CRIMINAL JUSTICE SYSTEM

IN

ENGLAND AND WALES

Gordon C Barclay

Third Edition

London
Home Office
1995

First Published: 1990 by Helsinki Institute for Crime Prevention and Control

Second edition: 1993

Third edition: 1995

ISBN 1-85893-259-9

Published by the Home Office, Queen Anne's Gate, London SW1H 9AT

List of Illustrations

1.   INTRODUCTION

1.1   Historical differences in how the legal system has developed within the individual countries which make up the United Kingdom have meant that England and Wales (together), Scotland and Northern Ireland should be looked at separately. The current paper only attempts to cover England and Wales, briefly setting out the criminal justice system as it operates at the end of 1994.

1.2   Government statistics show that:

- In 1993, 51.4 million out of a total United Kingdom population of 58.2 million, lived in England and Wales;

- About three-quarters of the population live in urban areas which make up 14 per cent of the land area;

- 5.5 per cent (3.0 million) of the population of Great Britain (England, Wales and Scotland) are from ethnic minority groups. The largest ethnic group is of Indian origin (840 thousand), followed by Black Caribbean (500 thousand) and Pakistanis (477 thousand). Together these three groups make up 60 per cent of the total ethnic minority population;

- In 1993, 10.2 per cent of the working population in England and Wales were unemployed.

2. HISTORICAL DEVELOPMENT OF CRIMINAL LAW AND PROCEDURES

2.1   The present legal system in England and Wales traces its origins back to the twelfth century, and the rapid expansion of institutions which followed the conquest of England by Duke William of Normandy in 1066. Before that time, there were differences of detail, particularly of procedure in each of the thirty-two counties into which England was divided. Unlike the rest of Europe, where countries based themselves on Roman law, the system of English common law, as it was called, developed uniquely. This system was based upon two principal courts, the Commons Bench and the Kings Bench. Around 1200 saw the appearance of a class of professional attorneys who were allowed to represent their clients in litigation. The system however, was centralised and this had to be reconciled with the need for local investigation and trial. There developed therefore, the major court of common law (the 'assizes') and it was not until 1972[1] with the introduction of the Crown Court, that these institutions were finally abolished.

2.2   Within Wales, a separate legal system had grown up and even after the invasion of Wales by Edward I of England in 1304, no attempt was made to substitute English for Welsh law. It was not until 1535 that Wales was finally incorporated into the common law framework. In Scotland, a system based upon Roman law developed. Following the merger of the Parliaments of Scotland and England and Wales in 1707, no attempt was made to unite the two systems and so both systems develop today side by side.

2.3   The law in England and Wales may be divided into two, namely:

a) The Common Law, which is made up of those general customs which have been regarded as laws in the land from time immemorial. The Common Law develops following the decisions of the higher courts.

Certain rules of conduct have by custom become laws, and offences under these laws are termed common law offences. A substantial proportion of Common Law is termed Case Law, built up from historical precedents.

b) The Statute Law, which includes all the laws made by direct order of the State and set out in Acts of Parliament (statutes) or subordinate legislation made under the authority of these acts. Many offences which were originally Common Law offences have been dealt with by an Act of Parliament; an offence can be both a common law and a statutory offence, although often common law offences are abolished by statute.

2.4   The other agencies of the criminal justice system are much later in origin than courts or the legal profession. The Police and Prison Services were set up nationally in the last century, the probation service at the beginning of this century and the Crown Prosecution Service as recently as 1986. Their present organisation is covered in detail later in this paper.

3. ORGANISATION OF CRIMINAL JUSTICE

3.1 GOVERNMENT

3.1.1 Three Government Department share responsibility for criminal justice within England and Wales.

a) The Home Office, which deals with matters relating to criminal law, the police, prisons and probation. The Home Secretary has also general responsibility for internal security.

b) The Lord Chancellor's Department, which deals with matters relating to the judiciary, administers both the Higher Courts (including the crown Court) and magistrates' courts and is responsible for Legal Aid. The Lord Chancellor is, as well as being the most senior legal official in the country, a member of the Cabinet and the Speaker of the House of Lords.

c) The Crown Prosecution Service, which is responsible for the independent prosecution of nearly all criminal offences instituted by the police. It is headed by the Director of Public Prosecutions and is under the superintendence of the Attorney General.

3.2 CRIMINAL JUSTICE COMMITTEES

3.2.1 A report by Lord Justice Woolf[2], drew attention to the fact that there was little local co-operation between criminal justice agencies. This has led to the setting up in 1992 of a national Criminal Justice Consultative Council and 24 Area Committees where matters affecting more than one agency can be discussed. The membership of these committees includes senior representatives of the police, probation service, crown prosecution service, prisons service, judges, magistrates and the legal profession. Both the Consultative Council and area committees are chaired by the judiciary.

3.3   POLICE SERVICE

3.3.1   There are about 127,500 police officers employed by the 43 forces in England and Wales. Just over 2,000 of these officers are seconded to central services, regional crime squads and other inter-force units. In addition, police forces in England and Wales employ just over 55,000 civilian staff, almost 5,000 of whom are traffic wardens who handle parking offences. Offences committed on trains or at stations are handled by the British Transport Police and the Ministry of Defence (MOD) Police handles MOD establishments. In addition, there are a number of forces, such as the Royal Parks Police, whose officers have defined territorial powers.

3.3.2   Each of the regular police forces in England and Wales is maintained by a police authority[3]. Outside London, the authorities comprise local councillors and magistrates; under the provisions of the Police and Magistrates' Courts Act 1994, the new police authorities will also include independent members. In London the authority for the Metropolitan Police is the Home Secretary and that for the City of London Police is a committee of the Corporation of London and includes councillors and magistrate members.

3.3.3   Police authorities are financed by central government grants and a precept on the council tax. Subject to the approval of the Home Secretary and to regulations, they appoint the Chief Constable. In England and Wales they are responsible for publishing annual policing plans and annual reports, setting local objectives, setting the budget and levying the precept. The Home Secretary is responsible for the organisation, administration and operation of the police service. He makes regulations covering matters such as police rank, discipline, hours of duty and pay and allowances. All police forces are subject to inspection by HM Inspectors of Constabulary, who report to the Home Secretary, and whose reports are published.

3.4 THE SPECIAL CONSTABULARY

3.4.1 Each police force also has a Special Constabulary, a part-time volunteer force. Special Constables have full police powers within their force area and undertake regular officer's routine policing duties when required, thus freeing regulars at times of emergency for those tasks which only they can perform. There were 20,566 Special Constables in England and Wales at the end of 1993.

3.5 COURTS

3.5.1 Ninety-six per cent of criminal cases are dealt with summarily at a magistrates' court. This is defined as a court of summary jurisdiction or justice acting under any justice or justices of the peace.[4] Such a court acts in a petty sessional court-house for a petty sessions area, although further court-houses may be set up. The case may be tried either by at least two (usually three) justices (lay magistrates) or by a stipendiary (a legally qualified and salaried) magistrate who sits alone[5]. Justices are appointed by the Crown (retiring at the age of 70) and receive no salary (only expenses). They have not usually had legal training before appointment and generally have full-time jobs in other walks of life. Magistrates' courts other than youth courts (and family proceedings courts) are normally open to the public. Justices are normally restricted to ordering sentences of imprisonment of not more than 6 months or fines not exceeding £5,000. For offences triable-either-way (see paragraph 4.3) if a more severe sentence is thought necessary, the offender may be committed to the Crown Court for sentence. Magistrates' courts in England and Wales are divided into just over 500 petty sessional divisions, each independent and under 105 local Magistrates' Courts Committees.

3.5.2 A report[6] has advocated the setting up of an administrative structure for the magistrates' agency. However, this has been rejected by the

Government. Alternative proposals[7] formed the basis of measures contained in the Police and Magistrates' Courts Act 1994, which are designed to re-organise the courts under a significantly lower number of local Magistrates' Courts Committees - justices clerks will continue as legal advisers to magistrates' and as court managers, but justices' chief executives will manage court committee area staff and resources. A Magistrates' Courts Service Inspectorate was established in January 1993 and placed on a statutory footing by the Police and Magistrates' Courts Act 1994. Its purpose is to inspect the administration and management of the magistrates' court service, in order to improve performance and disseminate good practice.

3.5.3   Within the magistrates' courts, certain are designated as Youth Courts. Such a court is composed of specially trained justices and deals only with charges against and applications relating to children and young persons. It should in most circumstances only deal with persons under 18 who are not jointly charged with adults[8]. It sits apart from other courts and is not open to the public. It consists of not more than three justices, including one man and one woman, or one stipendiary magistrate.

3.5.4   In 1972 following the Courts Act[1] the courts of assize and quarter sessions were replaced by a single Crown Court with power to sit anywhere in England and Wales. It is part of the Supreme Court. The Court has jurisdiction to deal with all trials on indictment and with persons committed for sentence, and to hear appeals from lower Courts, including juvenile cases. The Act imposed no geographical limitations on the catchment area of Crown Court centres, with County and district boundaries having no statutory significance in determining where a case should be heard. In practice most Crown Court cases are heard at the centre most convenient to the magistrates' court which committed the case for trial. The more serious offences can be tried only by a High Court judge, others may be dealt with by any circuit judge or recorder. There are currently about 90 court centres of the Crown Court divided into 6 regions, known as Circuits.

3.5.5 The Court Service becomes an executive agency of the Lord Chancellor's Department on 3 April 1995. From that date, the administration of the Crown Court will be the responsibility of the Court Service. Responsibility for policy issues on the magistrates' courts and judicial appointments remain with the Lord Chancellor's Department.

3.5.6 The Higher Courts include the Supreme Court which consists of a) the Court of Appeal; b) the High Court and c) the Crown Court. A person convicted at a magistrates' court may appeal to the Crown Court, while a person convicted at the Crown Court may appeal to the Court of Appeal and finally to the House of Lords. Appeals on points of law and proceedings arising in the magistrates' courts are dealt with by the Queen's Bench, Divisional Court of the High Court. It has very limited jurisdiction in such matters arising in the Crown Court. The highest court in the land is The High Court of Parliament or the House of Lords. This court is composed of the Lords of Appeal, who are lawyers of eminence generally appointed from amongst the judges of the Court of Appeal. On appointment they are made life peers and are thus members of the House of Lords. They deal with points of law of general public importance brought before them on appeal from the Supreme Court.

3.6   PROBATION SERVICE

3.6.1 There are 55 probation areas in England and Wales. In each area, there is a probation committee. The majority of those on these committees are justices drawn from the local courts, but persons are co-opted from other fields as well.

3.6.2 There were about 7,650 probation officers (whole-time equivalent) at the end of March 1994. This includes staff who supervise community penalties imposed on adult offenders, including probation, community service, and combination; and supervision orders for offenders aged 10-17. Probation officers also prepare pre-sentence reports for consideration by the courts.

Under the provisions of the Criminal Justice Act 1991, young offenders and adults sentenced to 12 months or more in custody, are supervised by the probation service before and after release. Adults sentenced to less than 12 months maybe supervised on a voluntary basis. About 10 per cent of field work resources of probation officers is on family court welfare work in connection with separation/divorce proceedings. Revised national standards covering the main areas of probation service work are being introduced, after careful discussion with services and all the other interested parties. Over 600 probation staff are seconded to Prison Service establishments, where they work alongside Prison officers and other specialists to confront offending behaviour and to maintain continuity between the custodial and community parts of the sentence.

3.6.3 HM Inspectorate of Probation, a departmental inspectorate within the Home Office, examines and reports on the performance of area probation services.

3.7 PRISON SERVICE

3.7.1 The Prison Service is an executive agency of the Home Office[9]. With 38,900 staff and an annual budget of £1.6 billion, it is one of the largest 'Next Steps' agencies yet established. Its Director General is responsible for the day-to-day management of the Service and is directly accountable to the Home Secretary for its performance and operations.

3.7.2 There are about 130 prisons in England and Wales, which perform a wide variety of functions. These include high security 'dispersal' prisons for the most dangerous prisoners; local prisons for men and women; closed and open training prisons for men and women; closed and open young offender institutions (for sentenced prisoners under the age of 21) and remand centres. Grendon is run as a therapeutic community.The present rules governing the running of adult prisons were initially laid in 1964[10,11]; those for young offender institutions in 1988 in the Young Offender Institution Statutory Rules[12].

3.7.3   The prison population has been rising rapidly in recent years. From a low of 40,600 in December 1992, there were around 50,000 prisoners in custody at the end of 1994. The prison population is expected to reach 55,000 by the year 2000.

3.7.4   To cope with the rising population, the Government has embarked on a major prison building and refurbishment programme. 21 new prisons have been built since 1980, providing 11,285 new places at a cost of £1.2 billion. Another six new prisons are to be built in the next few years.

3.7.5   As a result of this programme - the most ambitious since Victorian times - prison conditions have been made substantially more acceptable. 95% of prisoners now have access to sanitation at all times, and 'slopping out' is planned to be eliminated altogether by February 1996. The practice of 'trebling' - holding prisoners three to a cell designed for one person - has also been ended. Many other facilities have been extensively modernised and upgraded, including physical security and control rooms.

3.7.6   The Prison Service publishes a Corporate Plan, which sets out strategies and priorities over a three year period, and an annual Business Plan, which sets out key targets and a programme of work for the year ahead.

3.7.7   The Service's primary duty is to keep in custody those committed to it by the courts. The Service also has a duty, set out in its Statement of Purpose, to look after prisoners with humanity and help them live law-abiding lives in custody and after release. These various tasks and responsibilities are identified in the Service's six principal goals. The first of these is to protect the public by holding prisoners securely in custody. The other five are to:

a) maintain order, control, discipline and a safe environment;

b) provide decent conditions for prisoners and meet their needs, including health care;

c) provide positive regimes which help prisoners address their offending behaviour and allow them as full and responsible a life as possible;

d) help prisoners prepare for their return to the community; and

e) deliver prison services using the resources provided by Parliament with maximum efficiency.

3.7.8 The Service's priorities for the next three years include:

- improving physical security and security procedures, particularly at establishments holding high security prisoners, and reducing the number of escapes from prison and escort outside prison to a minimum;

- implementing incentive-based regimes in which prisoners are expected to earn extra privileges through hard work and responsible behaviour.

3.7.9 The private sector is becoming increasingly involved in providing prison services. Four prisons are now being managed by contractors and the six new prisons which are still to be built will be designed, constructed, managed and financed by the private sector. The Court Escort Service in England and Wales, which is taking over responsibility from the police and Prison Service for escorting prisoners to and from court, is being progressively contracted out.

3.8 CROWN PROSECUTION SERVICE

3.8.1 Up until 1985, the main prosecuting authority was the police. The Crown Prosecution Service[13] (CPS) was introduced initially in Metropolitan areas and by October 1986, it was set up across England and Wales, divided into 31 areas. However, a number of forces had, in anticipation of the creation of the CPS, begun to re-organise their prosecution arrangements, creating central administrative or operational support units with responsibility for preparing cases for prosecution. The CPS has 111 local offices (branches) which are responsible for the conduct of all police-initiated prosecutions (save for certain minor traffic offences to which a defendant pleads guilty). On 1 April 1993, the 31 areas were amalgamated into 13 larger areas, including a single area covering London. Each area is headed by a Chief Crown Prosecutor and comprises of a number of branches headed by a Branch Crown Prosecutor. Given the size of the new areas, these would normally encompass a number of police force areas. There are also Headquarters buildings in London and York. The CPS is under a statutory duty to take over the conduct of criminal proceedings instituted by the police. Each case that the police send to the CPS is reviewed to make sure that it meets the tests set out in the Code for Crown Prosecutors. If there is insufficient evidence to provide a realistic prospect of conviction or it is considered that a prosecution is not in the public interest, the CPS has the authority to discontinue or otherwise terminate the proceedings.

4. PROCEDURES WITHIN THE CRIMINAL JUSTICE SYSTEM

4.1 DETECTION AND CHARGING

Following the detection of an alleged offender for a crime, the options open to the police are:

4.1.1 No further action - the police may decide to take no action because they consider there is insufficient evidence to prosecute or that an informal warning may be sufficient. This will include cases where the suspects are children under ten years who are below the age of criminal responsibility[14]. Such children may be dealt with under the civil law, for example, through the use of care proceedings under the Children Act 1989.

4.1.2 Cautioning - Where an offender consents and admits his guilt, there is sufficient evidence for a conviction and it does not seem to be in the public interest to institute criminal proceedings, a formal caution may be given by, or on the instructions of, a senior police officer. Although frequently used for youths and first time offenders, it has recently increasingly been used for older offenders. A Home Office Circular (18/94) in March 1994 discouraged both multiple cautions and the use of cautions for serious offences.

4.1.3 Fixed penalties - The police may issue a fixed penalty notice for a wide range of motoring offences. Unpaid notices are registered as a fine by magistrates' court without any court appearance.

4.1.4 Charging - When an accused person is charged, the law requires that he is brought before a magistrates' court as soon as possible. He may be held in custody by the police to appear as soon as practicable. A person may also be released on bail, this is either before charge, when the bail is 'bail to return to the police station' , or after charge, when the bail is 'bail to the court'. Finally, a person may be summoned to appear at court, where they will be released without charge and not on bail. Warrants may only be issued where (a) the offence is triable only on indictment (see paragraph 4.3), or is punishable with imprisonment or (b) the address of the accused is not sufficiently established for a summons to be served. No branch of the executive or the judiciary can direct a police officer or the Crown Prosecution Service to bring criminal proceedings (or not to do so) in a particular case -this includes Ministers of the Crown.[15] The introduction of the Crown Prosecution Service during 1986, has meant that the power to continue with a prosecution or to discontinue proceedings, when appropriate, is now separate from the powers of investigation, arrest and charge invested in the police. It is now for the Crown Prosecutor to review, in accordance with criteria set out in the Code for Crown Prosecutors (revised in June 1994), all charges brought by the police (except for specified minor offences), and he has the right under section 23(3) of the Prosecution of Offences Act 1985 to discontinue court proceedings. Grounds for discontinuance are that it is felt that the evidence is insufficient to give a realistic prospect of conviction or that to proceed would not be in the public interest. Crown Prosecutors or agents acting on their behalf, conduct prosecutions at magistrates' courts; while at the Crown Court, cases are presented by barristers instructed by the CPS. Before 1986, many criminal cases were prosecuted by the police or solicitors/barristers acting on their behalf.

4.2   REMANDS

4.2.1 A magistrates' court may adjourn a hearing at any time and remand the defendant either in custody, or on bail. Also, when committing a defendant for trial or sentence to the Crown Court, a magistrates' court will do so on bail or in custody. Under the Bail (Amendment) Act 1993, the prosecution may, in certain circumstances, appeal against the decision by a magistrates' court to grant bail. The appeal is to a Crown Court judge and must be made within 48 hours. There is a statutory right to bail under the provisions of the Bail Act 1976[16]; but this may be denied in specific circumstances; namely where the court has substantial grounds for believing that if a defendant were remanded on bail, he or she would fail to surrender to custody; commit an offence while on bail; interfere with witnesses; or otherwise obstruct the course of justice, but also for the protection of the defendant. The Criminal Justice and Public Order Act 1994 provides for the automatic custody of those charged with, or convicted of, homicide or rape where the defendant has a previous conviction for any of those offences (unless a previous conviction of manslaughter or culpable homicide led to a non-custodial sentence). Where the defendant appears before the court accused or convicted of an offence allegedly committed on bail, the court need not grant bail. A magistrates' court has the power to remand a defendant in custody for up to 8 days in the first instance but thereafter, may remand him for up to 28 days, provided that the defendant is present in court and has previously been remanded in custody for the same offence (section 128A of the Magistrates' Courts Act 1980).

4.2.2 A person who is summoned or released on bail, may fail to appear on the day. Where there is no good reason for this failure to appear, he is said to have absconded and the court will issue a warrant for his arrest. In the case of a person failing to appear at the Crown Court after being granted bail, a bench warrant may be issued.

4.2.3 In addition to the general grounds for refusing bail, a youth under 17 may be refused bail if the Court is satisfied that he should be kept in custody for his own welfare. Youths refused bail must be remanded to local authority accommodation. There is an exception in the case of 15 or 16 year old boys who meet certain conditions. These are that the defendant is charged with a violent or sexual offence or one punishable in the case of an adult with imprisonment for a term of 14 years or more; or, that the defendant has a history of absconding while remanded to local authority accommodation and is charged with or has been convicted of an imprisonable offence alleged or found to have been committed while he was so remanded; and in either case, that the court considers that only a remand to a remand centre or prison would be adequate to protect the public from serious harm from him.

4.3 CATEGORIES OF OFFENCES

4.3.1 Three separate types of offences are defined[17] with offences either:

a) Triable only on indictment, which are the most serious breaches of the criminal law and are triable by a judge and jury at the Crown Court. These 'indictable only' offences include murder, manslaughter, rape and robbery.

b) Triable-either-way, which may either be tried at the Crown Court or a magistrates' court. Criminal damage is triable either way, if the value is £5,000 or greater (£2,000 until implementation of the Criminal Justice and Public Order Act 1994); otherwise it is summary.

c) Summary, which if proceedings are instituted are triable only at a magistrates' court. This group is dominated by motoring offences, for which fixed penalties can be issued.

4.4 PROCEEDINGS AT MAGISTRATES' COURTS

4.4.1 About 1,950,000 defendants are prosecuted annually in magistrates' courts; 480,000 for indictable offences (including triable-either-way), 580,000 for summary non-motoring offences and 900,000 for summary motoring offences. If the Crown Prosecution Service considers there is insufficient evidence such that there is not a realistic prospect of conviction or that this is not in the public interest, it may exercise its power under section 23 of the Prosecution of Offences Act 1985 to discontinue the proceedings at any time before the start of the trial. It may alternatively consider that the available evidence supports a different charge. The Crown Prosecution

Service discontinued about 175,000 cases in 1993.

4.4.2 About one in five indictable offences (including triable-either-way) are committed annually for trial or sentence to the Crown Court. Under the Criminal Justice and Public Order Act 1994, the process of committing cases to the Crown Court for trial is to be replaced by a transfer for trial procedure (this new procedure comes into force in mid-1995). Cases will be transferred for trial where:

a) a person is charged with an offence triable only on indictment;

b) a person is charged with an offence triable either way and either the magistrates' court decided that the offence is more suitable for trial on indictment or the accused does not consent to being tried summarily.

4.4.3 A defendant may also be committed to the Crown Court for sentence if the offence is triable either way and the court feels that a sentence should be given above its limits, i.e. over six months imprisonment and/or a £5,000 fine.

4.4.4 Before the case is transferred for trial in the Crown Court, the accused will be able to apply to the magistrates' court to dismiss one or more of the charges. In such circumstances, the court must consider the written evidence and any oral representations permitted and decide whether there is sufficient evidence to put the accused on trial by jury for the offence(s) charged. If not, the charge(s) must be dismissed. Where the accused does not make any application for dismissal, the case against him or her will be transferred without any consideration of the evidence.

4.4.5 For a triable-either-way offence, magistrates have to decide whether to try the case themselves or to transfer the case for trial to the Crown Court. The magistrates must decide whether they consider the case is too serious to be dealt with summarily. If the magistrates feel the case may be tried summarily, the defendant may still exercise his right to be tried by jury and the case can be transferred for trial. Nearly two-thirds of triable either way cases are tried in the Crown Court at the magistrates' decision.

4.4.6 Frequently an accused person will be charged with several offences, some of which are triable either way and others summarily. If the triable-either-way offences are transferred for trial, certain specific summary offences[18] may also be included on the indictment, ie: driving while disqualified, common assault and taking a motor vehicle without authority, but the Crown Court may only deal with them in the manner in which a magistrates' court could have dealt with them.

4.5   PROCEEDINGS BEFORE MAGISTRATES

4.5.1 On summary trial the court, if the accused appears, will tell him the charge and ask him whether he pleads guilty or not. If he pleads not guilty after hearing the evidence from the parties, the court must convict the accused or dismiss the case. If the accused pleads guilty, the court may convict him without hearing evidence. If the prosecutor appears but the accused fails to appear as requested, the court on proof of service of summons may proceed in his absence or adjourn the hearing or in certain cases, issue a warrant for his arrest. If the accused appears but the prosecutor does not, the court may dismiss the case or adjourn the trial. Where the offender is convicted, the court may proceed to sentence immediately or may adjourn if further information is required before sentencing. Defendants may be invited to plead guilty by post and therefore avoid a court appearance[19].

4.6   TRIAL BY JURY

4.6.1 A jury consists of 12 persons called at random from the list of all those persons aged 18 to 70 who registered as electors and are neither ineligible nor disqualified. These jurors take an oath to "faithfully try the defendant(s) and to give a true verdict according to the evidence". The duty of the jury is to listen to the evidence and to give their verdict whether the accused is guilty or not guilty. The accused has the right to challenge any juror for cause but he may no longer challenge without cause[20]. The verdict of the jury in criminal proceedings need not be unanimous but must be at least 10 to 2. If guilty, the judge of the court pronounces sentence. If convicted, the offender may appeal to the Court of Appeal and may have a further appeal to the House of Lords. The court may order the accused if convicted to pay the whole or any part of the costs incurred to be paid to the prosecution. The court may also, on acquittal, order the payment of defence costs from the central funds.

4.7   PROCEEDINGS INVOLVING YOUNG PERSONS

4.7.1   Young people aged between 10 and 17 inclusive, are mainly dealt with in the youth courts comprising specially trained magistrates. The youth court was introduced from 1 October 1992[21] and replaced the old juvenile court which dealt with offenders only up to and including age 16. In such courts, no person is allowed to be present, unless authorised by the court, except for the members and officers of the court, parties to the case, (normally including parents/guardians) their legal representatives, witnesses and bonafide representatives of the media. Proceedings may be reported in the press but the young person may not generally be identified. A child or young person is tried in the youth court regardless of his alleged offence unless he is charged with homicide (ie: murder or manslaughter) when he must be transferred or committed to the Crown Court for trial. A child or young person may be committed for trial in the Crown Court if charged with an offence for which an adult could be imprisoned for at least 14 years, charged with indecent assault on a woman, or is charged jointly with another aged 18 or more when both may be dealt with in an adult court. The new arrangements introduced for 17 year olds from October 1992, do not apply to some pre-trial purposes (i.e. in relation to police powers and remands) where 17 year olds will continue to be dealt with as adults.

4.8   SENTENCING

4.8.1   Under a statutory framework for sentencing introduced in the Criminal Justice Act 1991 (and amended by the Criminal Justice Act 1993), courts are generally required to impose sentences which are commensurate with the seriousness of the offence or offences committed by the offender. The Act does not attempt to define 'seriousness' and the Court of Appeal has provided guidance on interpretation since the Act came into effect in October 1992. In deciding what sentence to impose, the judge or magistrate will take account of :-

a) The facts of the offence, which have been presented in court, including any aggravating or mitigating factors. In addition, a defendant pleading guilty may wish to admit other similar offences and such offences may be often taken into consideration for the purpose of sentence without the offender being formally convicted of them and with no separate penalty being imposed.

b) The circumstances of the offender. In the Crown Court, the prosecution will provide a statement known as 'the antecedents' covering details of the offence, previous convictions and sentences. In addition, for more serious offences, a pre-sentence report giving fuller information will usually be prepared for the court by a probation officer. This report contains information about the character, personality and social and domestic background of the defendant; educational record and information about employment (if any), assessment of impact on victim and risk of re-offending. This report will include a proposal as to what community sentence (eg. probation order) would be most suitable for the offender if the court was to decide that such a sentence would be appropriate.

c) Plea in mitigation. In more serious cases an offender will be represented either by a barrister (counsel) or by a solicitor. The defence lawyer will make a speech in mitigation on behalf of the offender to give the court the defendant's explanation of the offence and any other matters going in the defendant's favour.

4.8.2 The principal penalties are:

a) Imprisonment - adults

Imprisonment is the most severe penalty ordinarily available to the courts who have the power to impose a sentence up to a maximum term specified by the Act of Parliament which created the particular offence. Under the Criminal Justice Act 1991, a custodial sentence can only be imposed if the offence is 'so serious' that only such a penalty can be justified for the offence or to protect the public from serious harm from a violent or sexual offender (or where an offender has refused to consent to a community sentence). The maximum custodial penalty reflects the gravity of the worst possible case and is thus high for the most serious offences, eg: life imprisonment for murder (for which it is mandatory), rape, robbery or manslaughter and 14 years for domestic burglary. A magistrates' court may not sentence to more than six months (or less than five days) for any one offence and to longer than 12 months in total, where sentences are being imposed for two or more triable-either-way offences and are to run consecutively. Where an offender is sentenced to imprisonment for several offences, the sentences may be ordered by the court to run either consecutively or concurrently. There are a number of factors which a sentence will take into account when deciding whether sentences should be consecutive or concurrent. Consecutive sentences will generally be appropriate, for example, where different types of offending behaviour is concerned.

b) Custodial penalties for young offenders

The use of all penalties for young offenders has declined in recent years as the range of available community penalties has increase and sentencers' confidence in them has grown. The Criminal Justice Act 1991[22] applied the same statutory criteria to young offenders as to adults. The 1991 Act and the Criminal Justice and Public Order Act 1994 made a number of further changes in the custodial sentencing arrangements for young offenders. For example, there is a common minimum age of 15 to both boys and girls for the imposition of a sentence of detention in a young offender institution; the minimum period for which young offenders of either sex aged 15 to 17 may be sentenced to detention in a young offender institution is two months and the maximum is two years and for young offenders aged 18-20, the minimum is 21 days and the maximum is the same as the adult maximum for the offence.

The aim of a young offender institution is to prepare the offender for his or her return to the outside community. A flexible but coherent programme of activities is provided, aimed at assisting the offender to develop personal responsibility, self-discipline, physical fitness and to obtain suitable employment after release. Youth of compulsory school age must receive a minimum of 15 hours education a week. Vocational training and work form an important part of the regime for older inmates. Links with families and the community are maintained as far as possible.

Youths aged 10 to 17 years convicted at the Crown Court of offences carrying maximum sentences of 14 years or more imprisonment in the case of an adult, may be sentenced to be detained for up to the adult maximum[23]. Although the offence of indecent assault on a female carries a maximum penalty of 10 years, this offence is included within the scope of this legislation, as are, for 14-17 year old, the offences of causing death by dangerous driving and causing death by careless driving while under the influence of drink or drugs. Detainees may be held either in Prison Service establishments or, if assessed as being suitable, in the local authority secure or open community homes or one of the two youth treatment centres.

The Criminal Justice and Public Order Act 1994 introduced a new type of order, the Secure Training Order, to deal with persistent juvenile offenders. Under this order, young people aged 12 to 14 years may be sentenced to be detained in a new system of secure training centres. It is expected that there will be five centres, each with about 40 places. The maximum sentence will be two years and sentences will be determinate, with half spent in custody and half in the community under supervision. The order will be available for offenders who have been convicted of three or more imprisonable offences; who have re-offended during, or been found in breach of, a supervision order; and, whose offending is so serious that only a custodial sentence can be justified. Current plans are for the first centre to open in 1996.

c) Life imprisonment

Life imprisonment, or its equivalent, must be imposed on all persons age 10 and over convicted of murder. It is also the maximum penalty which a court may pass for a number of the most serious crimes, including manslaughter, robbery, rape, buggery, assault causing grievous bodily harm, aggravated burglary and certain firearms offences. For these offences, the court may choose instead to impose a determinate prison sentence of any length or a non-custodial penalty.

A life sentence is wholly indeterminate. There is no entitlement to release at any stage but offenders may be considered for release on licence. For those serving a mandatory life sentence, release may only be authorised by the Home Secretary on the recommendation of the Parole Board and after consulting the Lord Chief Justice and, if available, the trial judge. For discretionary lifers (that is offenders who receive life sentences as a maximum, rather than mandatory sentence), the procedures changed with the implementation of section 34 of the Criminal Justice Act 1991 in October 1992. A court sentencing a person to life imprisonment for an offence other than murder, is able to specify a term after which the prisoner should be eligible for the new release procedures. A discretionary life sentence prisoner will be entitled to require the Home Secretary to refer his or her case to the Parole Board, if the Home Secretary has not already done so himself, when the relevant part has been served. The Board will have the power to direct the Home Secretary to release the prisoner on licence if satisfied that it is no longer necessary for the protection of the public that the prisoner should be confined. The Home Secretary will have no residual power as in the case of mandatory life sentences, to reject a recommendation by the Parole Board. These arrangements apply to prisoners of all ages, including young offenders.

Anyone found guilty of murder committed when under the age of 18 must be sentenced to 'detention during Her Majesty's pleasure'.[23] A person aged under 18 convicted of an offence other than murder for which a life sentence may be passed on an adult, may be sentenced to 'detention for life'[24]. A person convicted of murder who is aged 18 or over at the time of the offence but under 21 on conviction must be sentenced to 'custody for life'. This is also the maximum penalty when an offender aged 18 but under 21 is convicted of any other offence for which an offender aged over 21 would be liable to life imprisonment. Release procedures are the same as those for offenders over 21 described above.

All life sentence prisoners are initially released under the supervision of a Probation Officer. The reporting conditions of the licence may be lifted after a period of time, during which the individual has demonstrated that such restrictions are unnecessary.

d) Suspended sentence adults (aged 21 and over) only

Where the court decides that the offence seen in the light of the adult offender's record is sufficiently serious to justify a sentence of not more than two years imprisonment, the sentence may in certain circumstances, be suspended for at least one year and not more than two years. The suspended prison sentence is not served at all, unless the offender commits a further imprisonable offence during its operational period. The Criminal Justice Act 1991 further restricted the use of the suspended sentence of imprisonment to cases where the court takes the view that there are exceptional circumstances which justify its suspension. When passing a suspended sentence, the 1991 Act also requires the court to consider whether it would be appropriate to impose a fine or make a compensation order at the same time.

e) Community Sentences

The Criminal Justice Act 1991 increased and strengthened the range of punishments which are available in the community. They are now regarded as penalties in their own right and not as alternatives to custody. A community sentence can only be imposed when the offence(s) is 'serious enough' to warrant that penalty. The restrictions on liberty imposed by a particular order, must be commensurate with the seriousness of the offence and the most suitable for the offender. The main options are:

(i) Community service orders

An offender 16 or over who is convicted of an offence for which a court can send an adult to prison, may be required to perform unpaid work on behalf of the community. The offender's consent is required and such orders involve a minimum of 40 hours and a maximum of 240 hours to be completed within 12 months. The work is under the direction of a community service organiser, working within the probation service. If the order is revoked, the offender may be re-sentenced for the original offence. A wide variety of work is done including, for example, outdoor conservation projects, building adventure playgrounds and painting and decorating houses and flats for the elderly or handicapped.

(ii) Probation and supervision orders

An offender aged 16 or over who consents, may be sentenced to a probation order for a period ranging from six months to three years. A court may make a probation order in the interests of securing the rehabilitation of the offender; protecting the public from harm from him; or preventing the commission of further offences. Each offender must be supervised by a probation officer but the court has the power to include any other requirement considered appropriate. This could include residence, activities, attendance at a probation centre, treatment for a mental condition and treatment for drug or alcohol dependency. Probation centres, that run courses which offenders may attend for up to 60 days as a requirement of a probation order, are also available in a number of areas. For a young person aged 17 or under, an equivalent order called a supervision order may be set for periods up to three years. The supervisor for such orders may either be a probation officer or the local authority (in the person of a local authority social worker). A wide range of requirements may be attached to the order relating to accommodation and activities.

iii) Combination order

This order was introduced in October 1992 by the Criminal Justice Act 1991. It combines elements of both probation supervision and community service and may be given to any offender aged 16 or over. The maximum duration of the probation element of the combination order is three years and the minimum, 12 months. When a combination order is made, probation supervision continues for at least as long as community service is being performed. The minimum number of community service hours is 40 and the maximum 100. In 1993, about 9,000 such orders were imposed.

(iv) Other community penalties

Two further community orders are specified in statute. An attendance centre order may be made against an offender aged between 10 and 21 found guilty of an offence for which an adult my be imprisoned if an appropriate centre is available locally. An order will normally be for 12 hours, although offenders over 16 may be ordered to attend for up to 36 hours. Sessions at the centres are normally held on Saturday afternoons, with offenders required to participate in a structured programme of activities.

The Criminal Justice Act 1991 also made provision for the introduction of curfew orders. Such orders would require the offender to remain at a specified place for up to 12 hours a day for a period of up to 6 months. The Act allows for the monitoring of curfew orders by electronic monitoring of the offender's whereabouts. The provisions have not yet been brought into effect, although trials are planned for 1995 to assess the use of electronically monitored curfew orders as sentences of the court.

(f) Fines

A court may fine an offender for any offence (except murder or treason), although a court will not normally impose for more serious offences except in conjunction with another penalty. A system of unit fines was introduced in magistrates' courts by the Criminal Justice Act 1991[25] but difficulties with the system resulted in its abolishment in the Criminal Justice Act 1993[26]. The 1993 Act requires all courts to set fines which reflect the seriousness of the offence and which also take into account the financial circumstances of the offender.

Courts will usually allow offenders to pay the fine in regular instalments. The task of ensuring that payments are made is carried out by magistrates' courts. Where appropriate, the court can have payments deducted at source from an offender's wage or issue a distress warrant to seize a defaulter's property. The final sanction is imprisonment, with the sentence length dependant upon the amount outstanding. In 1993, there were 22,600 receptions for fine defaulting; 14,300 of these were sentenced for up to two weeks in prison; 5,300 were sentenced for between two weeks and one month; and 3,000 were sentenced for over one month in prison. The average time actually spent in prison was around 7 days. Most of those imprisoned for default are unemployed, and the Criminal Justice Act 1991[27] extended the attachment of earnings principle to income support.

(g) Discharge

A court may discharge a convicted person either absolutely or conditionally, where the court takes the view that it is not necessary to impose punishment. An absolute discharge requires nothing from the offender and imposes no restrictions on future conduct. The majority of discharges are, however, conditional discharges, where the offender remains liable to punishment for the offence if he is convicted of a further offence within whatever period (not more than three years) that the court may specify.

(h) Compensation

The compensation order is of particular significance in cases involving death, injury, loss or damage, as courts are required to consider making an order in such cases, and to give reasons where no such order is made. A compensation order can be made in addition to any other sentence or order, or can be the only sentence imposed for a particular offence. A magistrates' court can order compensation up to a maximum of £5,000 per offence; there is no such limit in the Crown Court. However, courts are required to have regard to the means of the offender when deciding whether to make a compensation order and when deciding on its amount.

(i) Capital punishment

Capital punishment for murder was abolished in 1965[28] but it is still retained for treason and some miscellaneous offences. The death penalty has not been used since its abolition for murder in 1965.

(j) Other sentences

A range of other sentences are used; confiscation orders, exclusion orders and disqualification from driving. Although not a sentence, a convicted person may be made the subject of a bind-over (as may any witness or party appearing before the court).

4.9 APPEALS

4.9.1 In criminal matters, the Crown Court deals mainly with appeals by persons convicted in magistrates' courts against their conviction or sentence or both. Appeals may be limited to conviction only or to part of a sentence (eg. a compensation order or driving disqualification) and the Crown Court may, if it considers appropriate, vary all or part of a sentence. The Criminal Division of the Court of Appeal hears appeals in criminal matters from Crown Court. Courts are constituted by the Lord Chief Justice and Lords Justices assisted by High Court Judges as required. A further appeal may be made to the House of Lords where it has been certified by the Court of Appeal Criminal Division that a point of law of general public importance was involved in the decision. The Attorney General has the power to refer unduly lenient sentences for offences triable on indictment to the Court of Appeal[29]. This power was extended in January 1994 to certain triable either way cases.

4.10 EARLY RELEASE

General principles

4.10.1 The schemes stem from the recommendations of the Carlisle Review Committee[30] and were introduced from 1 October 1992 by the Criminal Justice Act 1991. They restore meaning to the sentence awarded by the courts whilst ensuring that most inmates receive some support on release to reduce the likelihood of re-offending. All inmates are eligible for release before the end of their sentence. These arrangements for the early release of determinate sentence prisoners apply to young offenders, including those detained under Section 53(2) of the Children and Young Persons Act 1933.

Additional days awarded

4.10.2 Remission has been abolished and loss of remission as a disciplinary sanction has been replaced by the award of additional days (AWAs). These will delay all release and supervision expiry dates. This means that eligibility for release for inmates in all schemes, will automatically be put back by any Additional Days Awarded (ADAs). Additional days will not extend the original sentence: i.e. they could only go up to the 100 per cent point.

4.10.3 For those prisoners sentenced after 1 October 1992, there are the following early release arrangements based upon sentence length:

a) The Automatic Unconditional Release Scheme (AUR)

Eligibility: All inmates sentenced to under 12 months. There is no selection; they are released automatically half-way through their sentence.

Supervision: There is no compulsory supervision except for young offenders who are subject to statutory supervision under a YOI licence for a minimum of three months, or until the offender's 22nd birthday if that is sooner.

At risk provision: All inmates will be 'at risk' until the 100 per cent point of sentence is means that if they are convicted of further imprisonable offences committed before their sentence has fully expired, the court dealing with the new offence may re-activate all or part of the period of the original sentence outstanding at the time the new offence was committed, in addition to any new sentence (custodial or otherwise) it may impose.

b) The Automatic Conditional Release Scheme (ACR)

Eligibility: All inmates sentenced to 12 months or more but less than 4 years. There is no selection process; they are released automatically half-way through their sentence on a licence (issued on behalf of the Home Secretary by the Governor).

Supervision: They are subject to compulsory supervision up to the three-quarters point of sentence. Some sex offenders may be supervised up to the 100 per cent point of their sentence at the direction of the sentencing judge.

Breaches of licence conditions: Inmates who breach their licence conditions will be dealt with by magistrates' courts They may fine them up to £1,000; recall them to prison for a maximum of six months or the outstanding period of their licence if that is less; or refer the case to the Crown Court to recall them for the outstanding period of their licence if this is longer than six months.

At risk provision: All inmates will be 'at risk' until the 100 per cent point of their sentence (in the same way as the AUR arrangements - see above).

c) The Discretionary Conditional Release Scheme (DCR)

Eligibility: All inmates sentenced to 4 years and over become eligible for release on parole at the half-way point of sentence. All cases are considered by the Parole Board at regular intervals until the two-thirds point of sentence. Those not selected for parole within this period will be released automatically on licence at the two-thirds point.

Decision making: For inmates serving less than 7 years, the Home Secretary has delegated the decision on release to the Parole Board. For prisoners serving 7 years and over, the Parole Board makes a recommendation but the final decision rests with the Home Secretary.

Supervision: All inmates will be supervised until the three-quarters point of sentence, whether they are released on parole or automatically at the two-thirds point. Some sex offenders will be supervised to the 100 per cent point at the discretion of the sentencing judge.

Breach of conditions: Recall to prison for breach of licence conditions is dealt with by the Parole Board.

At risk provision: All inmates will be 'at risk' until the 100 per cent point of their sentence (see AUR arrangements above).

5.   THE POSITION OF THE VICTIM

5.1   There is a generous Criminal Injuries Compensation Scheme to help those injured as a result of crime in Great Britain, whatever their nationality. It is the most generous of such schemes in the world. The basis of assessing compensation was changed on 1 April 1994, to make the scheme simpler for claimants to understand, easier to administer, and to make the costs of compensation more certain. Under the new arrangements (which, because of a legal challenge are currently being operated on a provisional basis), compensation is assessed on the basis of a tariff (or scale) of awards for injuries of comparable severity. Everyone sustaining a similar injury receives the same award and they get it more quickly and with less fuss than under the former arrangements.

5.2   Local victim support schemes provide help and guidance to individual victims of crime. The schemes cover 100 per cent of the population of England and Wales. There are also witness support schemes at Crown Court centres, offering a range of support services to witnesses and victims. All these schemes are supported by Home Office grant, provided through the National Association of Victim Support Schemes.

5.3   A Victim's Charter[31], published by the Home Office in 1990, sets out the rights of victims of crime and explains how they should be treated by the various criminal justice services. Some of these services have since published charters or sets of service standards of their own, for example, the Courts, the Crown Prosecution Service and individual police forces.

5.4   Where the Crown Prosecution Service does not prosecute an offender, victims are free to prosecute privately, though in practice few do so. Following conviction in the criminal courts, the courts can award either full or partial compensation. This can be the sole penalty, or it can be combined with other penalties. In 1993, magistrates' courts awarded compensation in about 14 per cent of cases and the Crown Court in about 13 per cent of cases.

6.   CRIME PREVENTION

6.1   The Government's policy on crime prevention is being developed on a broad front. At national level, an inter-Ministerial Group on Crime Prevention has been tasked with ensuring that Central Government Departments operate in partnership to achieve more effective co-ordination in the fight against crime.   Expenditure on crime prevention in its widest sense across Government Departments is estimated to have been £240 million in 1993-94 compared with £200 million in the previous year, an increase of 20 per cent.   That figures is additional to the estimated £6.2 billion public expenditure on the police in 1993-94.

6.2   The National Board for Crime Prevention links the police, business and other sectors in the community in a top level partnership, generating fresh ideas, and spreading best practice.

Partnership

6.3   At local level, the Government takes the view that partnerships between the police, business, other organisations and the public are the best way to tackle crime. There have been many successful partnerships between the police and other local organisations, for example through the Home Office Safer Cities, initiative now a part of the Single Regeneration Budget. The Partners Against Crime initiative, launched by the Home Secretary in September 1994, is designed to get more individual members of the public, not just organisations, involved in crime prevention. There are three elements to the initiative. Crime concern hope to increase Neighbourhood Watch by 50% form its current 130,000 schemes in England and Wales, covering 5 million households. Street Watch, takes the Watch idea of using eyes and ears out into the street in a structured and organised way. Street Watch members are ordinary citizens with no police powers. If they spot anything suspicious, they report it to the police. Neighbourhood Constables are Special Constables but operating only in their own neighbourhood to which they bring a visible police presence.

6.4   The Police and Magistrates' Courts Act 1994 lays the foundation for a new partnership between the police and the public to tackle crime and create safer communities. In future, police authorities will be expected to draw up local strategies for building effective partnerships between local communities and the local police force.

Crime Concern

6.5   Crime Concern was set up by the Government in 1988 as an independent crime prevention organisation to stimulate the development of local crime prevention activity and to encourage good practice through initiatives such as Neighbourhood Watch schemes and Crime Prevention Panels. Other work includes consultancy services for local agencies and support for local partnerships. It obtains its funding through business sponsorship and through an annual grant of £500,000 from the Home Office towards its core expenses. Crime Concern organises local and national events (including the National Neighbourhood Watch Conference) and is at present developing Youth Action Groups/Junior Crime Prevention panels in schools across the country. There are 640 of these groups, in addition to 500 adult Crime Prevention Panels.

7. ROYAL COMMISSION ON CRIMINAL JUSTICE

7.1   A Royal Commission was set up in March 1991 to undertake a major review of the criminal justice system in England and Wales. The Commission, chaired by Viscount Runciman of Doxford, reported in July 1993 and made 352 recommendations. The Government made an interim response in February 1994 recording the current position in relation to 308 of the recommendations which were primarily for consideration by Government. It gave its priorities as the avoidance of miscarriages of justice; ensuring a proper balance in criminal procedure between the interests of the prosecution and the defence; making the process of justice more rational and less of a game played to arcane rules; improving the position of victims and other witnesses; achieving maximum efficiency in the use of available resources; and speeding up as far as possible, the delivery of justice.

7.2   The Government has currently accepted in principle, in whole or in part, 131 of the 308 recommendations addressed to it, all of which have either been implemented already or are in the course of being implemented. 159 recommendations are still being considered. In particular, a consultation paper was issued in March 1994 about the setting up of the independent Criminal Cases Review Authority which the Commission recommended should take over from the Home Secretary, the responsibility for considering alleged miscarriages of justice and deciding which cases it would be appropriate to remit to the Court of Appeal. Legislation to give effect to this recommendation will be introduced early in 1995.

8.   CURRENT STATISTICAL TRENDS (Table 1)

Table 1   The operation of the criminal justice system in England and Wales, 1983-1993 : key indicators

	1983	1986	1991	1992	1993
Notifiable offences recorded by the police (thousands)	3,247	3,847	5,277	5,592	5,530
- cleared up %	37	32	29	26	25
Persons found guilty or cautioned[1] (thousands)					
- aged 10-17	205	176	138	144	130
- aged 18-20	99	91	97	97	91
- aged 21 and over	271	252	281	298	295
Use of fines(%)[1]	43	39	35	34	34
Use of custody(%)[1]					
- aged 14-17	13.9	12.9	9.0	9.4	10.2
- aged 18-20	17.5	20.1	14.2	14.0	15.7
- aged 21 and over	17.0	19.2	16.5	16.1	16.1
Average prison population(thousands)					
- Unsentenced	10.7	10.1	10.2	10.1	10.7
- Sentenced	33.3	36.6	35.4	35.4	33.3
- Non criminal	0.6	0.2	0.3	0.3	0.6
Average sentence length[2] (months)	16.6	18.3	20.5	21.1	21.8

(1) Indictable offences only

(2) Adult males at the Crown Court

A.   OFFENCES RECORDED BY THE POLICE

8.1   The main measure used of the amount of crime with which the police are faced, is statistics on notifiable offences recorded. However, offences may either not be reported to the police or not recorded by them. From the 1994 British Crime Survey[32] based upon interviews with households, estimates suggest that the increases in actual crime have been lower than recorded by the police with only one-quarter of all crime recorded by the police.

8.2   In 1993, the police recorded 5.5 million notifiable offences of which 94 per cent were against property, 5 per cent were violent and the remaining 1 per cent were other types of crime. The total number of crimes recorded in 1993 was 1 per cent lower than in 1992. This was the first fall in the annual figures since 1988 and compares with a 5.5 per cent annual average increase over the last ten years.

8.3   Offences of theft account for one half of recorded notifiable offences, and the most frequent types of theft are of, or from, motor vehicles, which account for over a quarter of all offences. Offences of burglary, mainly involving property of small value, account for a further quarter.

8.4   There were 295,000 violent crimes recorded in 1993, of which 70 per cent were violence against the person, 20 per cent were robberies and 11 per cent sexual offences. Offences of violence against the person increased by 4 per cent in 1993, compared with 7 per cent in 1992. However, over 90 per cent of such offences were minor woundings. Sexual offences rose by 6 per cent in 1993, although rapes rose by 12 per cent. The increases in rapes are thought partly to result from a higher proportion of allegations of rape being recorded as crimes.

8.5   In 1993, 25 per cent of all offences were cleared up by the police compared with 26 per cent in 1992 and 32 per cent in 1986. For offences cleared up in 1993, 46 per cent resulted in an offender being charged or summoned for an offence, 15 per cent in a caution, 14 per cent were offences taken into consideration, 17 per cent followed interviews with convicted prisoners and 9 per cent where no further action was taken.

Fig.1 Notifiable offences recorded by the police England and Wales

Number of offences

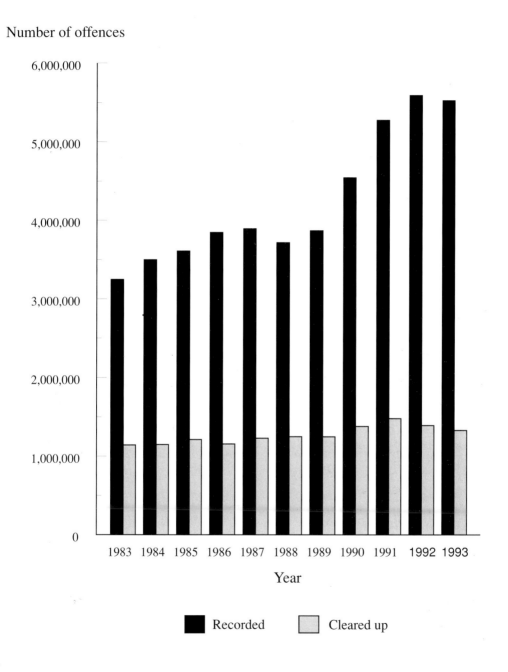

Year

■ Recorded   ▢ Cleared up

B.   OFFENDERS

8.6   The peak age for known offending was 17-19 years for males and 15 years for females in 1993. This is based upon the number of offenders either convicted by the courts or cautioned by the police for indictable offences, relative to population. In 1993, about 43 per cent of all known offenders were aged under 21. In that year, 73 per cent of juvenile offenders (aged 10-17) were cautioned, 34 per cent of those aged 18-20 and 29 per cent of those aged over 21 were cautioned. There has been a sharp rise in the number of persons cautioned over the past five years (for indictable offences the numbers rose from 136,900 in 1986 to 216,200 in 1992). A new Home Office circular issued in 1994 (sent out in draft in 1993) led to a drop in the numbers cautioned in 1993 by 3 per cent to 209,600.

C.   SENTENCING

8.7   Fines - The fine is the most frequently used disposal, 84 per cent of offenders sentenced for summary non-motoring offences and 91 per cent of those sentenced for summary motoring offences are fined. For indictable offences (including triable either way) the fine is still the most frequent disposal although it accounts for only 34 per cent of sentences. Since the early 1970's the use of the fine has fallen substantially for indictable offences.

8.8   Custody - Over recent years, there has been a substantial fall in both the numbers sentenced and the use of custody at magistrates' courts and the Crown Court. This fall was most significant for young offenders, where the number of those aged 14 and under 18 sentenced annually to custody, has fallen from 14,100 in 1983 to 3,900 in 1993 and for those aged 18 and under 21 where the fall was from 17,200 to 11,300. The use of custody in 1993 climbed back to pre-1991 levels after a fall in the fourth quarter of 1992, following the implementation of the 1991 Act.

8.9   Over the last few years, there has been a gradual increase in the sentence lengths awarded for the most violent offenders, including a rapid rise for rape offences from 4 years in 1984 to 6 years in 1988. Further recent increases have also occurred resulting from the use of non-custodial disposals for the less serious offences. For adult males at magistrates' courts, the average sentence length was just over 3 months in 1993 while at the Crown Court the overall average was 22 months. For burglary at the Crown Court, the average was about 16 months, robbery 48 months, violence against the person 22 months, and drugs offences 31 months.

8.10 Non-custodial - For those sentenced for indictable offences, about 10 per cent are sentenced to a probation order, 11 per cent to a community service order and 2 per cent a combination order; 22 per cent are given a discharge.

D.   PRISON POPULATION

8.11 The prison population has fluctuated considerably in recent years. The peak, 50,100 (seasonally adjusted), was reached in February 1988. Since then, there was a trough of 45,000 at the end of 1990, a peak of 47,700 in April 1992 and a trough of 42,200 in January 1993. Since January 1993, the population has risen, reaching 48,600 (July 1994). The average population in 1993 was made up of sentences prisoners (33,300), untried or unsentenced prisoners (10,700) and non-criminal prisoners (600). There was also about 5,000 sentenced young male offenders under the age of 21 in custody. The prison population contains a substantial proportion of foreign nationals of minority ethnic origin (5 per cent). In June 1993, after excluding all foreign nationals, 12 per cent of prisoners were of minority ethnic origin compared with 4.5 per cent in the population as a whole. Similarly, prisoners from the ethnic minorities made up 14 per cent of the remand population and 12 per cent of the sentenced population.

8.12 The seasonally adjusted prison population at the end of July 1994 was 48,600, this was 300 below the Certified Normal Accommodation currently available. A building programme is currently under-way to provide additional accommodation.

Fig 2.   Average prison population
England and Wales

Population

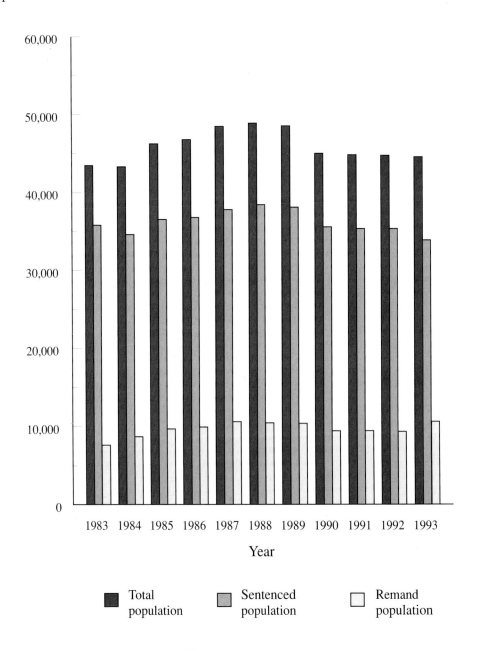

9.   RESEARCH AND STATISTICS PUBLICATIONS

Statistics

9.1   The following are the main annual publications containing statistics:

Digest 2, Information on the Criminal Justice System, Home Office
Criminal statistics, England and Wales, HMSO
Judicial statistics, HMSO
Prison statistics, England and Wales, HMSO
Probation statistics, England and Wales, Home Office
Report of Her Majesty's Chief Inspector of Constabulary, HMSO
Report of Her Majesty's Chief Inspector of Prisons for England and Wales, HMSO
Report of the Parole Board, HMSO
Prison Service annual report and accounts, HMSO
Report of the Criminal Injuries Compensation Board, HMSO

In addition, the Home Office publishes Statistical Bulletins covering regular and ad-hoc analysis on specific topics. Such bulletins are obtainable free of charge from Research and Statistics Department, Dissemination Unit, 18th Floor, Lunar House, 40 Wellesley Road, Croydon CR0 9YD, (Tel: 0181-760 2850)

Research

9.2   The Research and Planning Unit provides a service of research, information and advice to Ministers and policy division within the Home Office, Parliament and the public. The Unit's work covers a wide range of issues within the Home Office remit, with a large proportion focusing on crime and the criminal justice system. The publication and dissemination of research is an important and integral part of the RPU's work and the main publication outlets are:-

Home Office Research Studies
Research and Planning Unit Papers
Research Bulletin
Research Findings
Occasional Papers
Research and Planning Unit Programme

The main research reports are Home Office Research Studies (HORS) and Research and Planning Unit Papers. Recent publications in these series include:

Home Office Research Studies

No 125 - Magistrates' court or Crown Court? Mode of trial
decisions and sentencing, 1992.
ISBN 0 11 3410360. £6.25
Carol Hedderman and David Moxon

No 128 - The National Prison Survey 1991 -
Main Findings, 1992.
ISBN 0 11 341051 4. £7.60.
Roy Walmsley, Liz Howard and Shelia White.

No 129 - Changing the Code: police detention under the revised PACE
Codes of Practice, 1992.
ISBN 0 11 341052 2. £13.50
David Brown, Tom Ellis and Karen Larcombe.

No 132 - The 1992 British Crime Survey, 1993.
ISBN 0 11 341094 8. £15.00
Pat Mayhew, Natalie Aye Maung and Catriona Mirrlees-Black.

Research and Planning Unit Papers

No 66 - Juveniles sentenced for serious offences: a comparison of regimes in Young Offender Institutions and Local Authority Community Homes, 1992.
Jon Ditchfield and Liza Catan.

No 69 - Bail information schemes: practice and effect, 1992.
Charles Lloyd.

No 75 - Detention under the Prevention of Terrorism (Temporary Provisions) Act 1989: Access to legal advice and outside contact, 1993.
David Brown.

No 76 - Panel assessment schemes for mentally disordered offenders, 1993.
Carol Hedderman.

The Research Bulletin is produced bi-annually and contains a collection of short accounts of recent projects. Research Findings are summaries of published research.

Research and Planning Unit publications, with the exception of the Home Office Research Studies, are available free of charge, from Information Section, Home Office, Research and Planning Unit, Room 278, 50 Queen Anne's Gate, London SW1H 9AT. Telephone 0171-273 2084 (answer-phone). A full list of RPU publications is also available from this address.

Home Office Research studies can be ordered from HMSO Books, PO Box 276, London SW8 5DT. Telephone 0171-873 9090.

REFERENCES

(1)   Courts Act 1971, Chapter 23

(2)   Prison disturbances April 1990 : report of an inquiry by the Rt. Hon. Lord Justice Woolf (Parts I and II) and His Honour Judge Stephen Tumim (Part II), HMSO 1991 (Cm 1456)

(3)   s.1 Police Act 1964, Chapter 48

(4)   s.148 Magistrates Court Act 1980, Chapter 43

(5)   s.13-16 Justices of the Peace Act 1979, Chapter 55

(6)   Magistrates' Courts: report of a scrutiny, HMSO, 1989

(7)   A new framework for local justice, HMSO, 1992 (Cm 1829)

(8)   s.70 Criminal Justice Act 1991, Chapter 53

(9)   Report on the work of the Prison Service, April 1992-March 1993, HMSO, 1993 (Cm 2385)

(10)   Prison Rules 1964 - Statutory Instrument 388

(11)   s.47 Prison Act 1952, Chapter 52

(12)   Young Offender Institution Rules 1988 - Statutory Instrument 1422

(13)   Prosecution of Offences Act 1985, Chapter 23

(14)   s.50 Children and Young Persons Act 1933, Chapter 12 as amended by s.16 Children and Young Persons Act 1963, Chapter 37

(15)   Decision making in two English Police Forces, J B Morgan and D W B

(16)   Schedule Part 1 Bail Act 1976, Chapter 63

(17)   Criminal Law Act 1977, Chapter 45

(18)   s.40 Criminal Justice Act 1988, Chapter 33

(19)   s.12 Magistrates' Courts Act 1980

(20)   s.12 Juries Act 1974, Chapter 23 as amended by s.118 of the Criminal Justice Act 1988, Chapter 33

(21)   s.70 Criminal Justice Act 1991, Chapter 53

(22)   s.63 Criminal Justice Act 1991, Chapter 53

(23)   s.53 Children and Young Persons Act 1933, Chapter 12

(24)   s.8 Criminal Justice Act 1982, Chapter 48

(25)   s.18 Criminal Justice Act 1991, Chapter 53

(26)   s.65 Criminal Justice Act 1993

(27)   s. 24 Criminal Justice Act 1991, Chapter 53

(28)   Murder (Abolition of Death Penalty) Act 1965, Chapter 71

(29)   s.36 Criminal Justice Act 1988

(30)   The Parole System in England and Wales - Report of the Review Committee, Chairman: The Rt. Hon. The Lord Carlisle of Bucklow QC, HMSO 1988   (Cm 532)

(31)   Victim's Charter: a statement of the rights of victims of crime, Home Office,1990

(32)   Trends in Crime: Findings from the 1994 British Crime Survey, Research Findings No. 14 Home Office, 1994

FURTHER INFORMATION (Prison Service)

Further information about the work of the Prison Service, including copies of its current Corporate Plan , business Plan and Annual Report, is available from the Prison Service Communications Unit, Room 302, Cleland House, Page Street, LONDON SW1P 4LN (Tel: 0171-217 6633)